Power of Habit

The Truth About How to Change Your
Thinking Through Understanding
Motivation, What We Do & Why We Do It

Alexandra Masters

The Power of Habit
The Truth About How to Change Your Thinking
Through Understanding Motivation, What We Do &
Why We Do It
By, Alexandra Masters

First Published, 2013
United States of America

Special Thanks to You!

As a special thanks to you, our reader, please accept this FREE gift!

Motivation and Willpower Will Get Things Started But Only By Establishing Solid Habits Will You Be Able To Achieve Success! These **5 FREE E-Books** Will Show You How!

Download at:
AlexandSteven.com/signups/Power-of-Habit

DEDICATION

This book is dedicated to my father.
This book would never have been created without
him. He is the mentor to my success. My father is a
successful, caring, and loving businessman. He has
earned everything he has through hard work and
dedication. He learned from the masters of successful
habit development. I am blessed to be his daughter
and for the ability to follow in his footsteps. It's rare
to find a child with such wonderful parents.

I owe them my life.
Thank you Mom and Dad for all that you do and
have done to help me become the person I am today.
I know you will always be there for me and I will
always be there for you.

I love you two.
God has blessed our family and He has been a huge
factor in our success and decisions. We owe God
everything we have.

We work for Him. :)
Thank you God for helping me to create this book
and to share with the world the knowledge I have
gained through my trainings and experiences.

I am forever grateful.

INTRODUCTION

This planet is home to billions of people and trillions of creatures. Whether we observe a great king ruling over his land with an iron fist or a field mouse scurrying about the fields, each one of those that dwell on this floating rock we call home have one crucial trait in common - habits.

Rather than focus on the ways of the field mouse and the habits that its ever-so-interesting life exhibits, we're going to focus on a completely different beast - human habits.

Science has theorized that human habit originated during the time of primitive man; an adaptation to sustain our existence. You see, way back before you or I existed, when Man was more closely related to the animals that he hunted rather than those of us that walk upright, his mind needed a method of keeping himself alive.

As Man evolved, his primitive intellect developed a little trick. Whenever Man did something that the brain interpreted as "key to survival" it would release a chemical called dopamine into Man's system. Dopamine is referred to as the "good feeling hormone." Our brains release it whenever we do something that is interpreted as "key to survival." This is why you feel so great after an intense workout, acing an exam, or winning a competition.

When the brain of primitive man released dopamine into Man's system, it was because Man did something right – something "key to survival." Our primitive relative would then realize that what he had done was important. Naturally, he wants to feel the effects of his brain's dopamine release again, so he would complete the same task a second time. Then a third time. As he repeats this same process over and over again a habit forms.

Now, you're probably wondering how all of this applies to you. I mean, you're obviously not a hairy caveman after all. You're a person living in the hustle and bustle of today and a lot has changed since our days of foraging, hunting and gathering.

Although our lifestyles have changed, our habit forming processes have not. This poses a problem. If our habits were originally formed to help us survive, what happens when the life or death situation is taken out of the equation?

In essence, our brains get severely confused. How is your brain supposed to instruct you on what's right when we can consume processed foods and inject ourselves with drugs that make our brain's dopamine centers go haywire?

The brains of the 21st century are forming some seriously malicious habits and chances are, you've got some habits you aren't too proud of.

Are you following the crowd? Are you drinking every Friday and Saturday night because it's the "fun thing to do?" Are you doing what everyone wants you to do, rather than what you know you should be doing?

Are you living your life to its fullest or are you waiting for your life to be worth living? If you're waiting for your life to be worth living, you've got a serious problem. No one is going to make your life worth living but you.

What's a person of today to do? How do we break the cycle of bad habits we've developed? How do we replace them with beneficial ones? What's the most effective way to do so?

These are all valid questions that anyone who wants to change their habits, and their life, should be asking. For many, this book will be a turning point in their lives; the day they finally took their first step and performed the actions necessary to uncover their willpower and skyrocket their motivation to untold heights. This is the book that ends their search for habit reform.

Are you ready?

If you aren't, place this book back on the shelf. Don't worry, it'll still be here when you're ready to climb out of that hole and get your life back on the right track.

If you are ready to replace your bad habits, get your life back on track, and become the master of your own destiny, then the first step on your journey to life altering habit change is to understand exactly what you're up against.

So, what, exactly, are we up against?

PART 1: HABITS

Almost everyone knows that habits can have a large impact on our day-to-day lives, but do you know exactly what a habit is?

How are habits formed? Why do they have the impact that they do on our daily routine?

Why do people have bad habits? Habits are a fascinating physiological fact of life.

Let's explore it, shall we?

What is a Habit?

Simply put, habits are activities, usually simple ones, which are repeated on a schedule or as needed. There is more to a habit than just the activity though. There are a lot of psychological factors at play with habits. For instance, habits are often performed with little conscious thought.

One of the most important signs that a certain behavior is a habit is that there is little varied response.

That is, habits are performed the same way every time. Habits are thought to be a mental adaptation to ensure that when goals are met, we continue to use the same methods to meet those same goals in the future. After a while, the repetition of the action becomes an automatic response.

BUT HOW ARE HABITS FORMED?
Habituation is the process of forming new habits. One of the simplest ways to habituate a behavior is with a reward. The process of forming new habits with a small reward is so effective that it works with people as well as animals. In fact, people tend to form habits more easily than some animals because our psyche helps us correlate the cause and effect reaction much more rapidly in comparison to other creatures.

Rewards extend far beyond simple things like food. People can form habits for intangible rewards as well. Just the feeling that you have done well or accomplished something important can be enough psychological stimuli to help form habits.

In addition to rewards, repetition is key to forming habits. Repeating a behavior over and over makes that behavior more likely to become a habit. For instance, if you have a regular morning routine it's likely that at least part of the routine has become habit.

If immediately after waking up you head to the bathroom and brush your teeth, and you do so without thinking, you've just identified a habit.

WHY DO HABITS WORK?

Habits work because our brains seek to automate as much predictable behavior as possible. Hormones in the brain that cause feelings of reward are released every time a habit is performed. This ensures that the habitual behavior is more likely to be repeated again in the same circumstance.

WHAT ABOUT BAD HABITS?

We have all made a bad choice before, but some people seem to make them repeatedly. From drinking too much, to biting our nails or sleeping late, bad habits aren't as complicated as they might seem. Sometimes the reward that we get immediately from hitting the snooze button or having a drink outweighs any long-term rewards there may be associated with the habit. In essence, bad habits are a product of human laziness and our addiction to instant gratification. Most people would rather hit the snooze button and feel better now than to get up and prepare for a day of work to minimize stress later. In those cases, a harmful behavior can start to become a habit.

In the case of drugs and alcohol, the habit is often made by the addictive nature of the substances. Some drugs cause a large release of the same brain hormones that cause us to feel rewarded. Drug habit formation can be fast and is often times tragic.

Habitual behavior is a powerful thing. From little nervous ticks to keeping the dishes clean, habits are a part of everyone's life. However, with a little practice and reward, healthy habits can be encouraged and even the worse habits broken.

Are We Responsible for our Habits?

Though there are a few select members of society who live completely unpredictable lives, for the rest of us the concept of the routine reigns supreme. Basically defined, a routine is somewhat akin to a fixed program which has us performing the same actions day after day. Our routines are first hinged on the unavoidable responsibilities we have in life (such as eating, sleeping and working), and the holes in between them are filled with what we like to refer to as habits.

As defined in psychology, habits are behavioral routines we follow on a consistent basis because they occur subconsciously.It shouldn't come as a surprise that medical experts have been debating for a while whether or not we really are responsible for the habits we form; after all, with drugs, alchohol and the addictive additives contained within processed foods, can we really be blamed if they truly are formed in the uncontrollable subconscious level? In an attempt to solve this ageless mystery we will start by examining the two types of habits we can form, unintentional habits and self-inflicted habits.

Unintentional Habits

To begin, let us look into how habits can be formed without our knowledge. In most cases, these types of habits result due to the desire to fulfill a need over the course of a day. For instance, your job may give you a lunch break every day at the same time, which will lead you to form a habit of eating at the same place, at the same time, day after day. Because you were never planning on making it into a habit and it came to be because of the circumstances in which you have been placed, one could qualify such a habit as being unintentional. As such, it is possible to have habits formed without your knowledge.

Self-Inflicted Habits

Now we shall explore the other type of habit, the self-inflicted one. To define it as bluntly as possible, a self-inflicted habit results from one or a series of decisions which were made consciously with at least partial knowledge of the potential consequences. These types of habits often tend to border on various kinds of addiction and are usually the root of all bad habits.

For instance, you may have started overeating on a daily basis to cope with stress in your life, and it has come to the point where you keep on doing it even though you know it will bring you harm. If any kind of fault was to be assigned for the formation of a self-inflicted habit, it would rest on the affected person.

Putting Together the Big Picture

So, it has been determined that habits can be formed both with and without one's awareness. Everything really depends on the circumstances, for you can either be forced into a habit (making it unintentional) or force yourself into it (making it self-inflicted). It ought to be noted though that after a while, regardless of how your habit started out, it does end up lodging itself in your brain on a subconscious level, becoming an integral and automatic part of your life. It wouldn't be too far-fetched to believe in the idea that given enough time, all habits become unintentional.

Again, I ask you, are we responsible for our habits? For the most part, I would be inclined to say that yes, we are responsible for our habits because we choose which actions to commit to and which ones to abstain from doing.

There are times when we are truly powerless to influence our actions, but the majority of the time we simply need to remain alert, pay attention and think through the possible consequences of our actions.

The first and most important step to preventing a bad habit from forming (and to getting rid of one) is to recognize its presence, and then apply the golden rule of habit change: motivation.

Golden Rule Of Habit Change

Human beings are born with a natural desire to succeed in life. However, this success does not normally just come to us. It must be earned. Even though a few are born "successful", the majority of us have to toil for it.

Success and habit change is wholly dependent on motivation. There must be some force that drives the desire and will to succeed. Motivation is the flame within you that drives you to complete tasks and break the habits that require large amounts of effort and hard work.

For example, a student that is about to give up due to their dismal performance in mathematics can be motivated by themselves to improve. At school, this student may be convinced by fellow classmates to believe that he/she can never improve. The problem here is that a negative attitude is given an opportunity to be nourished.

Therefore, for this particular student to be able to improve in the subject, change in thought is mandatory.

In this specific situation, the student must focus his willpower on proving those against him wrong. If he cannot do so, he will fail. This is because our own thoughts are both our greatest obstacles and also our greatest assets in our journey toward achievement.

If this student were going to succeed, he or she would have to break the habit of poor performance. The student would need to dig deep within to muster the drive to succeed. This student must realize that no person is born a failure, that the only person that can make someone a failure is him or herself. The student must develop an "I can mentality."

Through constant guidance from experienced people and, more importantly, self-control, the student's attitude will begin to change. This attitude change must be accompanied by taking massive action.

Removing stumbling blocks may mean no more parties, no more staying up late, or any others which are contributing to the failure. It's study time. It's DO time. As success is achieved through this change in study, a liking of the subject can occur and if this is the case, the student's willpower will have become automatic. It will no longer take intense effort in study to succeed, the student's motivation will soar and success will be inevitable in this area.

On the other hand, some people fail to change their lives due to the fear of failure. They do not want to take risks. What if things don't work out? What if they look stupid? Generally, the greater the risks one takes in life, the greater the chances of success. By risks, I don't mean the 'go jump out of a plane or wrestle an alligator' type of risk. I mean speaking up at that meeting because you don't agree with the direction of the presenter or finally learning to surf because you want to despite your fear of sharks. It is worth noting that anytime a person experiences failure in life, great lessons are learned. This is because you must use your failure as a stepping stone to success and not see it as a barrier.

"If I find 10,000 ways something won't work, I haven't failed. I am not discouraged, because every wrong attempt discarded is another step forward."

-Thomas A. Edison, Encyclopedia Britannica

Fear is a word that has prevented people with potential from advancing their lives. Many refer to the word fear as an acronym, F.E.A.R. The acronym stands for False Evidence Appearing Real. It means that the reason you're afraid is not because of what you know, but because of what you think. The evidence for your thoughts is false, and you are wrong for being frightened. Don't let your fear stop you. Take the risk. Take action. Get out there and *do*.

Sometimes people let their negative past become a stumbling block in their lives. They never want to let go of that past experience that didn't go as expected. For you to be able to move ahead, you must appreciate the fact that today is different from yesterday. Today's experience will bring with it many new opportunities. Yes, some happenings may be unfortunate, but it is up to you to focus on the positives and continue bettering your life.

What's the best way to find the strength necessary to lose your fear, spark change, and ignite the fuse to change your stubborn habits? The answer to that question is two-fold: motivation and willpower.

Yes, we've all heard those words before, but let's see how to put them to actual use for ourselves.

Part II:

Motivational Willpower

Any person can choose whether or not he or she would like to do something. Human actions are necessitated by internal or external causes and the major internal cause of one's behavior is motivation.

But what lies behind motivation? In the following chapters you will begin to understand what makes you desire and the kindling beneath the bright, glowing flame of motivation.

What is Motivation?

Motivation is the process that triggers, guides and keeps up goal-based behaviors. It is what causes people to act; whether you want to reach for the remote to control your TV or read a book to learn.

It's what causes you to roll out of bed each morning, why your stomach aches when you're hungry and why your throat feels dry when you're thirsty. It engages the biological, cognitive, social and emotional forces that initiate behavior.

The term 'motivation' is used in everyday life to describe why an individual does something. For instance, you may say that a person is motivated to enroll for an IT certification program. Psychologists have come up with many different motivation theories such as humanistic theory, instinct theory and drive theory.

Motivation consists of three major components: intensity, persistence, and activation. Activation is the decision to kick off a given behavior, like enrolling in a class. Persistence refers to the effort geared towards achieving a goal even if there are obstacles like difficult tests, poor professors, or minimal time and resources. Intensity can be reflected in the vigor and concentration that is employed in pursuing a goal.

Types of Motivation

It is important for employers, teachers and other leaders to understand the basic types of motivation. A combination of internal and external factors encourages people toward autonomy and this enhances their self-confidence and sense of well-being. Workers and students who feel autonomous and confident would most likely work harder and attain greater results compared to their less-positive counterparts. The types of motivation, their benefits and drawbacks are as follows:

Intrinsic Motivation

Intrinsic motivation is the inner and deep inspiration which one engages in without expectations. In such a mindset, people do something because they think it's a good thing to do. They do it for the sheer joy and satisfaction. They are not interested in what they would get out of it.

For instance, a person can perform dance rehearsals the entire day not because he or she wants some recognition or wants to win a competition, but simply for the joy of dancing. It could be a person who volunteers at a soup kitchen simply to help out and feel as though they've done some good for the day. Whether difficulties arise or not during the course of their activities, they will persevere.

Intrinsically motivated people working together as a team encourage one another to perform the duties of their respective positions perfectly. They love the feeling of their own accomplishments and don't just rely on external rewards. Such people share their happy moments with their colleagues and are great team players. They have an infectious winning attitude that strengthens the team. These people are not concerned with the end product; rather, they are excited about the journey.

If you own a business you may be lucky enough to have hired an intrinsically motivated employee.

These individuals work to get internal gratification. Their work is result-oriented and this enhances their productivity. They set reasonable goals and are ready to take calculative risks. On the same note, having intrinsically motivated staff saves company money in terms of turnover costs. Such employees will be less likely leave their jobs or work less efficiently because getting external motivators like bonuses and rewards isn't their reason for doing well. Their hard work is driven by knowing that their team and superiors value their contribution. They feel useful, needed, and have a purpose.

Extrinsic Motivation
Extrinsic motivation is the inspiration based on external rewards. For instance, an extrinsically motivated student puts more effort into studies because he or she wants good scores. In this case, it does not matter whether he or she enjoys the course or not. The student has only one goal; to attain good grades and he or she will work hard even if the subject is hated. Extrinsically motivated individuals are goal oriented such that they are less concerned about their happiness or personal development. Their only aim is to achieve their goals.

Extrinsic motivation can change or vary according to the value of the external reward. Extrinsically motivated people can be unmotivated easily when there is no reward.

For instance, if an employee is told that she would not receive any incentive for extra contribution, she might not work harder. This is the distinction between intrinsic motivation and extrinsic motivation. It's not about the journey; it's about the end goal. The reward can be in various forms, such as verbal praise by telling an employee or a student that he or she did an excellent job, a letter or note of thanks, financial rewards such as bonuses, pay increases, paid vacations and other prizes, and peer recognition.

Introjected Motivation
Introjected motivation is from an internal, pressuring voice. This is the typical form of motivation experienced when forming new habits and breaking old ones. The motivation for action is triggered by shame, worry or guilt. It inspires a person to initiate an action through a sense of responsibility and obligation and not because they may want to. For instance, an introjectedly motivated person will go to church every week because of fear of the possible negative effects or being ridiculed by their peers even though they do not enjoy the church service in any way. This kind of motivation should be avoided as it cultivates anxiety. It should be the reason for deciding to break an old habit and form a new one; however, it should not be the only driving force.

Identified Motivation

This type of motivation comes with a sense of apathy. Let's say you want to be a writer but you don't really care for English class. You would be motivated to succeed in your English class because you realize and have identified the fact that succeeding in English class will provide you with the skills necessary to succeed as a writer.

Often confused for extrinsic motivation, identified motivation is centered on long term goals whereas extrinsic motivation is centered on the short term. The individual is not motivated by immediate rewards or guilt. He just recognizes that the action is beneficial to his advancement and accepts it as his own.

Strategies to Awaken Your Motivation

There are plenty of challenges that can force someone to lose enthusiasm and back down from goals. Since motivation is at the core of success, losing it spells out imminent failure as it blocks out positive attitude. People seeking motivation tend to get misled by the ideology that changing their overall state of mind or environment is the answer to their lowly situations. The truth is, amending external stimuli only serves to boost morale on a short-term basis when actual motivation necessitates a consistent drive.

In order to assuredly get motivated in your endeavors, you need to act accordingly:

#1: Ask for Guidance

In the Old Testament, when Moses was getting ready to take the Jews out of Egypt, the Lord instructed him to confront the Pharaoh. Each time Moses went to confront the Pharaoh the Lord "hardened his heart" and the Pharaoh turned Moses away. Only when the Lord "softened" the Pharaoh's heart was Moses permitted to leave Egypt with his people.

There is truly only one way to be successful in life and that is to practice God's word in your everyday life. Even if you aren't religious or are skeptical, consider this,

"If you live your life without God and he does not exist, then you and I will cease to be when we die; however, if you live your life without God and he does exist, what do you do then?"

Whether you believe or not, God only wants you to live a righteous life and spread his good word. If you ever need help, ask him. You know what they say,

Matthew 7:7 *"Ask and it will be given to you; seek and you will find; knock and the door will be opened to you."*

#2: Adopt a Positive Mentality

Motivation comes from within and is therefore a product of positive emotions and thoughts. Expectations may be cause for persistence in any task, but when the going gets tough, only belief and self-confidence can keep you going.

You need to carefully assess your thoughts by listening to what you tell yourself or others, and gauge whether you are positive or not. Your aim should be to highlight your strengths rather than undermine your chances.

#3: Lay Practical Goals

For you to overlook the challenge ahead and avoid getting overwhelmed, it will be apt that you formulate some rational targets. This is easier done by segmenting the workload into convenient parts so that you have mini-milestones on your way to the main goal.

If for example, you are working on breaking a bad habit, the immediate goal would be to figure out what happens exactly before the habit takes place. Once you identify the trigger, you can begin to formulate your next mini-milestone.

#4: Accept Your Situation

Quite a number of people fail miserably because they obstruct themselves from their visions. As much as they may set reachable goals, failing to realize their flawed state makes it hard for them to make changes happen. By keenly examining your current situation, you will notice the things that weigh you down as well as the strategies that do not work.

This is crucial since it helps in formulation of better techniques to approach your hurdles. More so, if you realize that the conditions of your situation are not favorable, you will promptly be able to seek help and enhance your chances.

#5: Take Charge

Being able to take absolute responsibility of your tasks considerably increases your odds of success. This is spot on because it helps you stay away from excuses that prevent you from doing what you are supposed to do.

Put together a list of the things that cloud your mind when you are presented with a challenge and analyze them critically to make the necessary changes. Coming up with an enforced timetable for tasks and habits can help you shun procrastination and time wastage.

#6: Incentivize

Ultimately, you should have reason to carry on by either rewarding or giving yourself positive reinforcement. The reward can be anything as long as it boosts your spirits and helps you optimize your mental vision.

Other than expecting to achieve, you should make a list of things that can work as payoffs for successfully completed chunks of work. These can be as simple as resting or getting a major treat.

By keeping these guidelines in mind, you can develop and maintain high levels of enthusiasm through life's hurdles and emerge as a true performer.

Now, what if I told you there was a part of the human psyche that could bring about results faster, and more powerfully than motivation?

What if I told you of a way to make your motivation, goal setting, and habit reform *automatic*?

Would you want to know?

Of course you would!

Motivation vs. Willpower

If motivation is the process that triggers, guides and keeps up your goal-based behaviors; if motivation is your desire, your want, your drive to do what you do, then what is willpower? Motivation and willpower, two words often used synonymously, are actually incredibly different. How, you ask? Well, willpower, simply put, is your natural, innate ability to motivate yourself. Willpower is the tinder to the flame that is motivation. It is what sets off motivation. It is the other half, the key, to unlocking your motivation and your habit changing abilities.

Before I explain, let's take a quick English lesson, shall we?

Willpower by definition is self-control: the trait of resolutely controlling your own behavior. That's a fact. Willpower and motivation are not synonymous; rather, willpower and self-control are. And it makes sense, doesn't it? I mean, if willpower is necessary to create that *drive*, that *push*, that is motivation then you are, in fact, *controlling your will*.

Another fun fact, willpower is also a compound word. Obviously, it comes from the words will and power.

The *power* to *will*.

Willpower is the power to will yourself, the power to motivate yourself, and the power to control yourself. Without willpower, an individual cannot have motivation. It's as simple as that. Every person on the planet has willpower. Every single one of us has the ability to control ourselves and create the motivation necessary to push ourselves in the direction of our goals, whether they are developing a new habit or breaking a current one. But, there is a common misconception when it comes to willpower and motivation.

Let's consider the following scenario with a man we'll call Frank.

Frank is overweight and lives alone. Frank does absolutely *nothing* day in and day out. He hits the snooze button for thirty minutes after it sounds in the morning when he is supposed to be getting up for work. After finally getting out of bed, Frank slips into a clean shirt (if he can find one in the pile of clothes on his floor), grabs a donut for breakfast, and drags himself to his 9-5 job (which he hates).

He does the minimum required; just enough to keep his supervisors off his back. He slacks off the majority of his workday. On his break, he hits the drive-through because he didn't wake up early enough to pack his own healthier lunch.

Finally, after hours of monotonous "work" and slacking off, Frank punches the clock and heads home to his beat up apartment. When he arrives home, he cracks a few beers, turns on the TV and slowly drifts off into an alcohol induced slumber. This sad state of affairs is the typical day in the life of Frank.

Now, based on this description of Frank, what would you consider him to be missing? Motivation or willpower? Would you believe me if I told you Frank was actually an incredibly motivated person? I know what you're thinking, "Alexandra, there is NO WAY that Frank is motivated. He doesn't do anything! He sits on his butt all day and does nothing to better his situation." Now hold on there, before you throw this book in the trash, let me explain.

You see, Frank and everyone else on this planet are motivated by a very basic need: survival. Yes, it's true that Frank does nothing to change his ways, but he still gets up for work every morning. He still goes to that job he hates to get that paycheck. He still drives to the liquor store to pick up his "hard earned" beer. Frank has lots of motivation. The motivation is what gets him to *do*.

If you reference back to the types of motivation in **"What is Motivation?"** Frank is filled to the brim with identified motivation. He realizes that getting up and going to work are necessary for his end goal of survival. If Frank wasn't motivated, he would never get out of bed. It's due to Frank's lack of a different resource that he can't get himself up and out of that dingy apartment in order to change his life.

What Frank is missing is *willpower*.

Frank doesn't have the willpower to deny himself that extra thirty minutes in the morning to get ready like a responsible adult. Frank doesn't have the willpower to keep from slacking off; to keep to his work and excel in his profession. And Frank, most certainly, does not have the willpower, the *self-control*, to deny himself from unhealthy meals like the breakfast donut, the drive-through lunch break, and the post-work six-pack.

It is because of Frank's lack of willpower that he is stuck in the miserable hamster wheel that is his life. Frank knows this, just like you know certain habits are bad, but he doesn't have the willpower to do anything about it because Frank is afraid of change. He's afraid of failing, afraid that it might be all for naught. Frank would rather live his rotten life than change it because he hasn't exercised his self-control in years. He's forgotten how to use it.

It's because of this, that Frank doesn't have the *power* behind his *will* to slow the hamster wheel down, step off, and begin building himself a better, more fulfilling life in a new direction. Though if he ever does, he should probably start with a salad!

Perhaps you're in a similar boat. Hopefully, you're in a better spot than our pal Frank here, but perhaps you too, can't seem to find the willpower you need to motivate yourself to do better, to break a bad habit, or to form a new, beneficial habit. Perhaps you're looking for a way to locate the source of your willpower so that you can skyrocket your motivation to heights you've never thought possible.

The key to utilizing your willpower and unlocking your motivation is to make your willpower **_automatic_**.

Making Your Willpower *Automatic*

Almost everything we do in our lives that has a lifelong value requires some sort of effort and many times involves some level of discomfort. We, as humans, are designed to avoid discomfort and oftentimes try to eliminate it, not embrace it.

Sometimes forming new habits is discomforting until you are past the process of forming the habit, and then it just is. When you are developing a habit into an integral part of your lifestyle, you are taken out of your comfort zone. It is not natural; it is not the norm for what you are used to doing. Even if you know it is a positive habit you are forming, it's still foreign to you.

Willpower and habit tie hand in hand. To develop a habit, your willpower must be strong. You have to be fully confident that you are capable of forming this new habit. If inside your head your thoughts are negative and you don't really believe in yourself fully, you've already failed. How do you expect to succeed with such an attitude?

Those who are successful at changing any habit or developing new habits go into the process with full confidence and no lack of faith. You must be confident that you are in control of your thought processes.

Let's say you want to develop a habit of eating less unhealthy food and more fruits and vegetables. There are those who, when beginning to implement a new habit, are intimidated by the challenge or don't believe they can achieve their goal. These individuals have failed before they have even begun. Often their friends have an unhealthy lifestyle and their family has an unhealthy lifestyle, so they automatically think they are doomed.

On the other hand, there are those who are sick of the way they have been acting, eating etc. and decide it's time for a change. They don't worry about what others will think, or if they will fail. They go for it with an internal confidence and succeed.

It's true; there will be times when you are uncomfortable. There will be times you want to quit. Remember, nearly anything in life that has value requires hard work and effort in earning. You must be willing to invest in yourself.

What habit have you been wanting to break? What habit have you wanted to make part of your daily life? Are you sick of worrying what others think? Are you working on too many things at once and not giving your new habit the attention it deserves?

Thoughts are actions. What you believe is going to happen, generally does, but you have to be willing to work. Only "thinking" about what you want to achieve in your life won't get you very far.

Your willpower is a very powerful thing. Strengthen it by not giving up so quickly. The more you do it, the more natural it will become. When you first wake up, embrace your new habit with a positive attitude. You will feel amazing each and every time you complete something that you don't want to do, but you must know it is important for yourself and maybe even for your family.

Things take time to become automatic in your everyday lifestyle. For example, a diet is nothing but a short-term goal. Eating healthy is a lifestyle.

The goal is to eventually no longer need willpower. Your habit should become so automatic that it would be weird if you were not doing it in your everyday routine. It should become secondhand nature. The willpower you must summon to coax the blossoming of a new habit will have become a habit in itself and will reinforce your lifestyle. You will desire performing whatever your new habit is and it will no longer be work.

When I first became serious about starting a healthy lifestyle, a lot went through my head. I'll be honest with you; my willpower was not fully charged. It was far from the automated process it is today.

I have loved sweets since I first learned to chew food. My dad would find me sitting in my crib shaking my rattle muttering to myself, "Candy in there? I think there's candy in there!"

I know what you're thinking, "That kid had issues." It's true, I did! I still do, but I have formed a habit that turned into a healthy lifestyle. Want to know exactly how I did this? I went from not being able to go a day (more like minutes) without some sort of candy or sweet to a full **month** without a single, delectable, morsel of sugar.

I made the decision that I wanted to stop eating sweets as much as I was and that I was going to start really living a healthy lifestyle in December of 2010. Some parents worry about their kids doing drugs, drinking alcohol, or smoking. My health-nut parents' only worry was where they would find the next stash of empty candy wrappers.

You see, my mom is a nutrition encyclopedia. She knows more about health than anyone I know. She has a gift, and you can only imagine how worried for her little girl she was. Then I got to an age that I knew better than to want to live on nothing but sugary sweets. I knew my habit was not only a bad one, but a very unhealthy one. So, I put myself to the test. I decided to quit sweets during the most difficult month of the entire year: The month of baking, cookies, parties, and junk food eating - December.

Challenge accepted.

My future, my health, my body and my family were more important to me than sugar so I used this to my advantage. I realized that although chocolate cake with buttercream frosting tastes like a one way ticket to Heaven for the moment, I worried about my future. What would happen when I'm 30 and have a family of my own? I don't want to have diabetes or be too overweight to go outside and run around with my children. They deserve better than that, and so does my body.

Sometimes habits are hard to form because we are so busy living in the moment. Think about where you will be in 10 years if you do not change the bad habit you have been dying to eliminate. Is it a scary thought? Think about where you will be in 10 years if you start developing a new, healthy habit today. I'm sure you will like that outcome much more. I'm confident in anyone being able to do what they set their mind to. That means I'm confident in you. It means I truly believe that you can break your bad habits and replace them with beneficial ones.

But I cannot control anyone or anything around me. I can only control myself. I didn't let the smell of the cookies I was baking for the Christmas party get in my way. I didn't get mad at anyone else who was eating in front of me. I didn't get aggravated about all the food I could be enjoying at this very second. I kept calm, I always asked God for His help in overcoming my battle.

As a matter of fact, I realized God controls everything. It is my belief that without asking for His help, I wouldn't be where I am today. God saw my determination and trust in Him to help me get through that month of sweets and He helped me every step of the way. He gave me life and I need to respect the body He created.

It was truly amazing to experience how easy it was to go a full month without not only no sugar, but junk food as well. Once I created that good habit and eliminated all the sugar, I became addicted to the success. I stopped eating unhealthy foods. I ate all raw, healthy, nutritious foods for a full month without cheating on my new lifestyle. My new habits started snowballing before me. It came to the point where I was no longer craving the sweets I had avoided during the day each night because it was no longer my lifestyle. I was in it for the long haul.

Nowadays, I have a "cheat day" once a week where I treat myself to eating a meal I enjoy guilt-free. Anything in moderation is not going to kill you (except maybe lightning strikes). Do I miss my sweets during the week? Yes. Am I glad I asked for His guidance and made the switch? You better believe it! It makes my "cheat day" so worth the wait.

It no longer requires any effort on my part to generate the willpower to keep my week clear of junk food. I would feel absolutely horrible about myself if I ate bad even twice a week, let alone the seven days a week I used to. I now enjoy doing what I used to hate and I'm incredibly happy with that change.

Thanks to my persistence during that crazy, cake-filled December, my habit of building up my willpower became ingrained within me and my willpower had finally become **_automatic_**.

PART III:

Change Through Motivation and Willpower

At this point you should be beginning to understand exactly what it takes to change those troublesome "hard to break" bad habits and the perfect balance of willpower and motivation in order to put your productivity and habit reform to the top of its class. But what else can we do to change our habits? How do we train ourselves to have stronger willpower? What if that habit is just too hard to break?

You have the questions. I have the answers. Read on!

Our "Self-Control" Muscle

Everyone seems to want to increase their self-control, but many people might not understand what it truly means to have it. They may want to quit their bad habit but they just can't resist. They need to find a way to strengthen their resolve, but what can they do? Advice for how people should go about doing this has changed over the decades, but the reality of what self-control actually is hasn't. There are some core strategies that do seem to work. Allow me to introduce you to what it means to have self-control, and how to get more of it.

Imagine that self-control is a muscle in your brain. Like any other muscle, you're going to need to work it out in order to build enough strength to take on certain tasks. Just as if you stop going to the gym, if you stop working out your "self-control muscles," they are going to weaken.

Before you try to use your self-control to quit something cold turkey, you're going to want to "pump some iron" with your "muscle" on that part of your brain. Think of these next steps as workout routines that will build some serious self-control "muscle."

Identifying Self-controlled Behaviors

The first thing you want to do when you want to improve your self-control is to simply think about the behavior you want to change. Many people get caught up changing their overall mindset, or their outlook on life, but often it is easier to simply change one thing that you do instead of redesigning your entire personality.

By simplifying things and making habit change less of a massive event and more akin to choosing between a red or blue shirt to wear for the day, you'll not only be working out your self-control "muscles" but you'll be boosting your confidence too.

Focus on the End Result

Another important aspect of training yourself to develop self-control is to simply give yourself motivation to succeed. For example, a strong reason people fail at dieting is that they lose sight of the reasons for why they started the diet in the first place. A diet may begin when people realize they are grossly overweight, or when a doctor recommends it to avoid heart disease. This may spur on some immediate action, but they will soon taper away from the diet plan after some time. Understanding why this happens is a core component of continuing to motivate yourself.

When we first get a glimpse of our bodies after we've gained weight, or hear an advertisement about smoking causing cancer, we may get an initial jolt of fear. This jolt of fear might cause us to take immediate action for a short time, but this is only happening due to the body's natural fight or flight reflex. This reflex is not long-lasting enough to permanently change the way a person controls his or her behavior. To continue motivating your dieting or other habit change, you'll have to find a way to reward yourself occasionally.

If you've had a great week dieting and notice that you've lost a few pounds, break from your routine and eat something that you really love. This won't break your diet completely because it will give you incentive to keep trying for the next week.

Set aside a "cheat day" that will let you splurge, but only if you've met certain criteria. You can do the same thing for trying to break or form other habits as well. Rather than quitting cold turkey, try to taper off so that you perform the bad habit less often.

Set Standards

You're going to want to set goals to make sure your self-control strategy is actually working. If you're on a diet and it's not helping you lose weight over a period of time, it may be time to change your diet plan. This same mentality should be applied to all habit change. If you're not hitting the mark, take a step back, reevaluate, and try again. Make sure that you set manageable goals, and definitely don't set the bar too high at first. But if you hit a few easy goals at a time, you'll be encouraged to keep on doing what it takes to keep reforming those habits.

Ultimately, it will be you who decides whether or not you develop the self-control necessary to change your life. It will take determination and effort, but most of the time you wanted to make these changes for a good reason. If the end result is that your life is improved, then you should not let anything get in your way. If you ever feel stuck or require guidance, ask Him for support. You'll be surprised just how quickly He will answer.

Breaking Tough Habits

As mentioned earlier, any kind of behavior that you have repeated many times becomes almost automatic and subconscious. A habit can be beneficial if it is a good habit; however, it could be just the opposite and with unbearable consequences when it is a bad habit.

Success in any part of life is hard to achieve with bad behaviors and choices. This is because bad habits act as unyielding blocks to your set goals. It might be your career, your marriage or any other part of your life; bad habits will always be poisonous and lead to frustrations and disappointments.

These bad habits could range from gossiping, procrastinating, thinking negatively about everything, seeking too much attention, being defensive, and/or popping pills as a method to deal with stress. With time, the bad habits in your life may take over and define your character, denying you great opportunities to prosper or achieve your goals and dreams.

So how do you break these bad habits before any real damage is done? These steps should free you from your bad habit blues.

Find the Bright Spots:
As previously discussed, every bad habit is hard to break mainly because it has become automatic. Any bad behavior that you have been doing for a period of time becomes encrypted into your unconscious and is triggered by a certain experience or chain of thoughts.

Automatic thoughts are rooted on past experiences so that when similar experiences recur, you automatically find yourself doing what you had said you would not do. Some of the bad habits you have are rooted in the good feelings you feel after you do them. This is because the bad habits you have trigger those chemical releases (dopamine) in your brain, which activate the brain's reward center.

Overcoming bad habits, therefore, may seem quite impossible, especially after several failed attempts.

However, one very important step in overcoming this is through finding the bright spots. Ask yourself, what do you stand to gain if you succeed in overcoming the bad habit? Are there any moments that you succeed in keeping away from the bad habits? How did you feel when that happened?

Trying to resist a bad behavior and failing could be devastating and lead to a great lack of motivation and willpower. When you find yourself in the bad habits once again, focus on the moment that you had victory and convince yourself that you can do it again.

Map out the Critical Moves:
In order to overcome a problem you must always understand the root cause of it. You should try to understand what leads to the bad habits- what are its roots? If you have the habit of sending emails on your Smartphone or chatting with friends through text messages while in a meeting, then you need to understand what triggers that. Could loss of interest be the issue? What really triggers that bad behavior? When you understand the cause of the problem or what leads you in to the bad habit, you will then find it easy to map out a way to overcome the habit.

This is where the critical moves come in; what you do immediately when the bad habit has been triggered is very critical since it will define whether you will overcome the bad habit at that particular moment or not.

Mapping out the critical moves will be of great help when it comes to putting the present obstacles in place and overcoming them. Some of these critical moves may be easy to execute while others may require some preparation. However, whether easy or not, critical moves require you to be well motivated, well knowledgeable and in control of the situation.

Point Yourself Towards the Goal:
The whole point of stopping bad habits is to achieve something- to become a better person, be more productive at work, have better relationships with your loved ones and so on. There is always something good that you want to achieve at the other end of the struggle. To achieve all of this you have to point yourself toward the main goal and continue going toward it at a rate that works for you.

After understanding the bad behavior, what triggers it, and avoiding the behavior one or two times, it is now a matter of deciding to quit the behavior for good. Of course, there are some bad habits that will take a longer time to overcome and there are some that you can easily overcome.

Either way, it starts with the simple steps of pointing yourself towards the main goal, understanding what you need to do to get there and focusing on the bright moments when you managed to avoid the habit and the good that will come out of you kicking it out of your life.

Shrink the Change:

Overcoming bad habits also involves making changes to the way you think and act when confronted with certain situations. This change might not be easy to adopt and, therefore, you need to shrink that change as much as possible in order to make everything easier and the transition seamless. This might consist of getting other people close to you involved so that you get all the help that is required to break the habit.

However, the main goal here is to make the change as comfortable as possible, and hence easy to adopt. This is a very basic step that will help you reach your goal faster. After some time, you will grow into the change and you will then have a very easy time resisting the bad habit.

Overcome the Obstacle:

At this stage, you are ready to overcome the obstacle. As you now know, there is always something that triggers subconscious thoughts that lead to the bad habit. Once you have directed yourself towards the goal and achieved complete understanding of what causes the bad habit, then you are ready to now face the problem and overcome the obstacle.

Again, it may not turn out to be as easy as you might have thought but keep yourself motivated and your willpower strong by focusing on the good and the end goal. You will overcome the obstacle through enacting the required changes to the way you react to situations.

Remember, going against what comes automatically requires effort, but it is very easy to achieve if you identify the habit.

Build-up the Habit

Bad habits have bad consequences; however, good habits have the opposite results. Overcoming bad habits requires making changes and these changes should develop into good habits.

For example, if you have overcome the bad habit of demanding too much attention, then the required change might have been to pay more attention to those close to you and to not be selfish. This change can result in the good habit of being a better person and also make you more likeable and easier to relate to due to your newfound consideration of other people's needs before yours.

You can then build on this new habit and end up benefiting each and every day through having strong, rewarding relationships.

Building up a new habit is crucial because you need something new that will replace the old habit. Something new is required to fill the vacuum and prevent you from falling back onto your bad habits.

Bad habits could be what are keeping you from achieving what you have always desired. However, developing good habits can help to counter this and enable you to achieve more than you had initially set out to do.

You *need* to break those bad habits. Breaking bad habits requires commitment and a complete understanding of the triggers and action of the bad habit. You must be moving toward a goal, shrinking the change, overcoming the obstacle and then, finally, building and reinforcing that good habit that will take its place.

This book has been an incredible stepping stone during your journey toward habit reform. You now have a choice to make; you must ask yourself:

"Do I continue going through my life the way I always have? Or am I going to take action, incite change, and get my life on the road to success?"

You know I'm rooting for you.

You've got the knowledge.

Now get out there.

Head out into the wilderness, and **DO.**

-Alexandra Masters

Need More Help?

As a special thanks to you, our reader, please accept this FREE gift!

Motivation and Willpower Will Get Things Started But Only By Establishing Solid Habits Will You Be Able To Achieve Success! These **5 FREE E-Books** Will Show You How!

Download at:
AlexandSteven.com/signups/Power-of-Habit

Made in the USA
Middletown, DE
05 April 2022

63658112R00045